Christmas
love y
Jakisha

12 TIPS TO WOW, INFLUENCE, AND COMMAND YOUR LIFE

TAKISHA
BROMELL

Copyright © 2018 Takisha Bromell
www.takishabromell.com

All rights reserved. No part of this publication may be reproduced or transmitted in any form or by any means without prior written permission.

ISBN-10: 198761710X
ISBN-13: 978-1987617108

DEDICATION

To my father, Webster Lewis Bromell
You are the real WOWSER in all of this. I love you Daddy!!!

While I was writing the first draft of this book, he was fighting for his life. God brought the inspiration for this book to help me get through that time. I couldn't sleep as I lay in his room at the hospital. I would write over night as he was resting so I could make sure he was all right. To see him now, living his life so strong and brave, all I can say is thank God!

Acknowledgements

Thank you, Lord!

So many people inspired me to dig deeper, think bigger, and go for it as I took my leap into entrepreneurship. In the process of creating my flight pattern, I would call them, have dinner with them, go to their homes, and every time I left one of them, I went away with a nugget of wisdom or another piece of the puzzle to consider.

Thanks to my Mastermind Group: You are my incubator. I never left you empty, but always left overflowing with ideas! Brianna Gaynor, Christie Wilson, Edwin McKnight, Sue Jeffers, Laura White Dahl, Jennifer Thibodeaux, Terence Hillsman, Michelle Froedge, Pastor Annie Flowers, Uncle Soji Tinubu, and Len Turner.

Thanks to my besties: You are my midwives. Every tear you wiped away I so appreciate. Ophelia Randolph, Diane Pimentel, Melonie McCallum, Miranda Middlebrooks, Jasmine Balom Murry, Cena Martin, Ramonda Newsom, and Jan Turner.

Thanks to Katrina Waldrip, Ruby Barnes, Catina Carney, Sandra Whitaker, Tammi Woods, Keaira Henderson, Ashlyne Huff, Cindy Nix, Belinda Arender, Patricia Vance for listening to my dreams!

My Manuscript Team: You are all Rockstars in my book! Lee Rennick, (editor and chief), Lindsi Solomon ("last eye" editor), and Lindsey Underwood (book designer). Thank you!

To my family and friends across the world, I love you! Smooches….

Last but not least, to my Aunt Gloria Bromell-Tinubu. As a little girl I always looked up to you. You are my WOWSER! I hyphenated my last name because of you (LOL!). Learning and education were important to me because of you. You are always blazing the trail, and for a little black girl from South Carolina I needed to see that from a strong, beautiful, vibrant, confident black woman from South Carolina. You encourage me to walk with my head held high with purpose, passion, and perseverance. Thank you!!!!

My Aunt Gloria and Me
(Not sure why you let someone take a photo of me with my hair like this (LOL), but even then I was right there at your side.)

Table of Contents

FOREWORD 10

INTRODUCTION 13

WOWSER TIP #1: WOW (Yourself) 19

WOWSER TIP #2: THINK (Exponentially) 29

WOWSER TIP #3: BE (Uniquely You) 39

WOWSER TIP #4: ENERGIZE (Your Space) 49

WOWSER TIP #5: DRIVE (Results) 59

WOWSER TIP #6: SEEK (Excellence vs Perfection) 69

WOWSER TIP #7: ACCELERATE (Forward) 77

WOWSER TIP #8: DON'T (Play it Safe) 87

WOWSER TIP #9: ENGAGE (People) 95

WOWSER TIP #10: LOSE (to Win) 105

WOWSER TIP #11: EXECUTE (Your Vision) 115

WOWSER TIP #12: WOW (God) 125

AFTERWORD 133

FOREWORD

As Takisha and I sat in the hospital waiting room together, frantically catching up since we had not spent any real time together in a long time, she said (with a twinkle in her eyes) that she was writing her second book. WOW! I was flabbergasted. I didn't know she had written her first book! So, she brought me a copy of that book, A Lady in Waiting, and, of course, after reading it, I said "WOW" again!

We were at the hospital because her dad, who is my oldest brother, had just had surgery to stop bleeding on his brain. As an only child having to care for her mother before her death, Takisha was adeptly managing the current situation with her dad -- with passion, proficiency, and a calmness that was awe inspiring. She stayed at the hospital and engaged the medical staff to make sure her Dad was getting the best care possible. However, even in the mist of all of that, she was writing her second book, WOWSER!

In writing this book, Takisha gives you a first-class seat on her personal journey to becoming a WOWSER. If you want to be a WOWSER, you can trust Takisha to show you how because that's who she is. She can show you how to become a WOWSER because she has been on that journey herself, and has arrived in living color.

This "twelve course meal" of a book is power-packed. It is full of all the nuggets you need to first "WOW Yourself," and then be able to think exponentially, be uniquely you, energize your space, drive results, seek excellence, and accelerate forward.

While positively pushing you forward, Takisha exhorts you by saying "Don't play it safe." At the end of the day, you must be willing to "Engage People," to "Lose to Win," and ultimately, to "Execute Your Vision."

After pouring all of who she is into this book so that you can drink fully, and become all of who you were purposed to be, Takisha ends the book with what is the beginning of it all for her -- her love of God. Wow!

Not only does Takisha allow you to drink from her fountain of WOWness, she provides you the opportunity to sip from the wisdom of other WOWSERs like Nelson Mandela, Napoleon Hill, Octavia Spenser, Lao-Tze, and Marianne Williamson. But she doesn't stop there!

She also gives you "Food for Thought" which allows you to "dig deeper" into who you really are, and then she encourages you with "Action Words" to become the WOWSER you were born to be.

But there's more! She helps you get creative with your thinking by proposing "Motivation Questions" that allow your juices to flow.

Finally, Takisha shares with you the "Insider Secrets" of other great WOWSERs! WOW...how great is that? She puts it all on the table for you to partake. So, you get to decide whether you will eat and come into the fullness of all of who you are, or if you will continue to walk through life malnourished and unfulfilled. Takisha and I choose fullness and we entreat you to join us!

When Takisha asked me to write this foreword, she truly WOWed me! While I've had a lot of "firsts" in my life -- the first in my family to go to college, the first African American to earn a Ph.D. in Applied Economics from Clemson University, the first African American woman to earn her party's nomination for Congress in South Carolina, etc., this is the first "Foreword" I have ever written for a book! It goes without saying, this is an exciting WOW-filled first!

I am deeply honored and delighted to have had the opportunity to write this foreword, and to be able to express my admiration for Takisha, our WOWSER, on behalf our family -- her Dad, her Mom, grandparents on both sides of the family, and hundreds of relatives all over the world! We love you and are so proud of you!

Love and Blessings,
Gloria Bromell Tinubu, Ph.D.
Georgetown, South Carolina

INTRODUCTION

Hello there dear friends,

Before you get started reading this amazing little book (shameless self-promotion), I believe it is important that you understand my fundamental belief system. I feel you need to know a bit about me, why I do what I do, the reason for this book, and how everything all ties together into the neat little package that brought about WOWSER.

I believe that 70% of people have no understanding of their purpose. This means that they are sleep walking through life. Sadly, these people will probably die with the regret of not taking the time to understand whom they are inside.

I believe that 20% have an idea of what their purpose is in life, but fear, life circumstances, and negative belief systems have them immobilized.

Five percent know what their purpose is and are primed, ready to pursue their dream, but they don't have a strategic plan in place. They believe they are under a glass ceiling.

Author Dan Sullivan calls this the "Ceiling of Complexity ™." As you succeed in life, you get to a place of inefficiency because you lack the ability to effectively solve problems created by growth. I believe that the Ceiling of Complexity™ requires foresight. You have to develop the instinct to find a new way of thinking in response. You can't advance and use the same tactics you were using, as you are now in a new place.

Newton's law says, "For every action, there is an equal and opposite reaction." In business, pushing beyond that "reaction" to change requires new thinking -- both critical and intentional -- new action planning, and execution strategies.

Then there is the final five percent. I think this is where we long to be. These are the people who live with no holds barred.

I am "finally" jumping into this group. I have taken the time to face my fears, accept or change my life circumstance, and purge the negative beliefs that have kept me from reaching for what I have always wanted. It is an absolutely amazing thing to see my dreams come true, and my purpose manifest. Why didn't I do this earlier? Why didn't I fully engage all of me before?

I recently wrote and self-published my first book, A Lady in Waiting. It helped me to see the desire that resounds in my soul, and what it is to be fully "Takisha." It helped me make decisions about what I wanted in life.

The experience of writing and releasing A Lady in Waiting; the love and support from family and friends; the positive feedback from you, my readers, is all -- WOW! It gave me courage to move forward. It made me ask myself, "What would it feel like, what would happen if I could live in the fullness of Takisha?

Let me explain what I mean by sharing a bit of my backstory. A few years ago I was working as a chief operating officer. It was a great job. I loved it. My passion in helping people find their purpose was never far from my thoughts, yet I had safely tucked it in the back of my mind.

But as I found success in my working for another, I couldn't keep my passion in the background any more. I decided I would start my own company, Purpose Innovators.

I shared that information with my boss. Instead of giving me support, he had a perplexed look on his face. Then he started to ask questions, "How would it affect my position and the company?" I stopped him. I said, "Wait a minute – you have me primetime. Sometimes for ten hours a day. And then there are the weekends. You get the best of me, when I am the most alert, focused, and dynamic."

After that conversation, I was uncomfortable. From then on I shared only snippets of my passion with the company. When I opened my first office, what should have been done with excitement, was done silently and covertly. I found myself shrinking back.

Now let's switch back to last year and the release of A Lady In Waiting. Even though I was working for another employer, I feared what my boss would think about what I saw as the most exciting part of my life, writing and self-publishing my first book. While I shared my book with him, he even wrote the foreword, I still felt uncomfortable being all of me. Sharing my whole truth with him. Being fully Takisha.

I have to be honest, as a professional, manager, and owner I understand the plight of an owner. I know how hard it is to invest in an employee, support their growth, and develop their skills only to say goodbye. But as the employee on the other side, I was slowly dying inside. I felt as if every advance in my life couldn't be fully celebrated.

As I was working on this book, I came to see that my passion would always play second fiddle to my primetime job if I kept the same course. My passion would never get my best self; I would always be moonlighting.

WOWSER was on pace to come out in record time. I wrote most of it over Labor Day weekend. I planned to release it on the second of December. Then I started worrying again, would I choose to shrink this book, too?

Suddenly it was December 10th and I was just working on edits, and adding ideas about reaching for what you really love. I was not fully living the life I wanted. I was not doing what I coached others to do -- what I so loved helping others do – take the leap towards my passion. I was not being fully Takisha.

What does the fullness of Takisha look like? Owning my business, controlling what I do, when I do it, where I do it, and how I do it. Spending the heart of my time working on projects that make my soul sing. Creating in freedom and with confidence. No shrinking back. No intimidation. Allowing love and passion to guide my life.

I realized that wanting isn't enough. NOW is my time to DO. That was my WOWSER moment, when I chose to DO. To activate the fullness of my gifts. My calling. My purpose.

I want to welcome you to the WOWSER REVOLUTION! I encourage you to take a moment and think about what the fullness of YOU looks like. What will it look like and feel like to be unequivocally, 100% YOU?

I am excited to introduce you to the concept of finding your purpose in a different way. Think of someone that you know who is dynamic, intriguing, living on purpose, and owning his or her life. I bet you have thought to yourself, how do they do it? How can I become more like them? How can I live my life fully, meaningfully, and on purpose?

This book is where I will share with you the world of a WOWSER. How does a WOWSER think? How does a WOWSER move? What are the secrets to a WOWSER's success? In the following pages I have included insider secrets that no one tells us.

I hope you enjoy reading about how to become a WOWSER. As you begin using these tips in your own life; I look forward to seeing you at the top, reaching for your life's dreams!

Blessings,
Takisha

WOWSER TIP #1:
WOW (Yourself)

"Why fit in when you were born to stand out!"
Dr. Seuss

I am my biggest critic. I can assassinate my ideas in one second flat.

But, then, when I think of something amazing, brilliance comes to the forefront, and there is this energy that bubbles up inside of me that can't be denied. My senses tingle. My synapses hum. I go into over drive. My eyes widen. I sit up straighter in my chair. I am ready to pounce on my idea like a dog with her favorite treat, and explore the idea further. My mind is totally captivated by my objective, and nothing else exists in the outside world until I have had time to fully ripen my inner thoughts. This is when I know that I have WOWed myself. My notebook comes out, and my brain drain begins as I put pen in hand to capture all the details.

The WOW Factor can come to anyone. Really! Becoming a WOWSER all begins with you. If you can't WOW yourself, if you can't captivate your heart first, how in the world will you WOW others and bring others with you? How will other people catch on and want to sing your song? Being a WOWSER is also about being a leader, using your leadership to accomplish your goals, and helping others accomplish theirs.

To be a WOWSER, you have to WOW yourself and say, "darn, that's good!"

That is how this book started. I took myself out to brunch and, as I sat there contemplating where to go next, the words WOW, WOW Factor, and WOWSER came to my mind. Only to have it instantly begin the assassination attempt; my brows started to furrow, and my mind said WHAT?? I said to myself, "What is WOWSER? What in the world does that mean?"

WOWSER was a word definitely not in my vocabulary. I immediately looked up the definition on my cell phone, and it said, "a person who is publicly critical of others, and the pleasures they seek; a killjoy". My furrow deepened. I was almost about to be a killjoy and kill this thought when I looked at it again. LOL!

I noticed that it was considered a noun. BUT, as WOWSER and WOW Factor coursed through my mind, I realized that WOWSER seemed more like an adjective. That intrigued me. It made me want to keep my inner thoughts going. If there were other possibilities for the word, I could create my own definition for it as a noun.

Seated at my table, my notebook came out, I wrote down the word WOWSER. As I contemplated the word, ideas started to cascade from my mind. Why couldn't the definition of WOWSER morph? Why couldn't I introduce this word in a new and meaningful way?

As I was editing this book, I was told about the word "wowzer." It means something of great interest or beauty, something worth saying "wow" about. This was closer to what I wanted WOWSER to mean, but still not exactly.

I knew that the word WOWSER (I like the spelling W-O-W-S-E-R) was destined to take on a new shape. Because I am going to be the one to lead the march to acceptance of the new definition. "Yes!" I said to myself, "it could morph because it had already transformed in my mind. It just needed to be refined, and marketed properly."

Here it begins. WOWSER, in my new definition, *means to WOW emphatically with purpose and resolve. To be the WOW FACTOR in your life and industry.*

So let me say, I WOWed myself when I wrote the definition. I felt the intensity of the moment when I started to birth the idea of this book. My senses heightened. I really don't know what I ate at the restaurant. I was totally captivated by my thoughts about WOWSER. They wouldn't let me go, nor did I let them go. Another book was forming. Ideas for chapters started to take shape, and for another 72 hours (the same time it took me to write the initial draft of A Lady in Waiting) I allowed my creative juices to flow and manifest.

With the completion of my initial draft of this second book, I WOWed myself. I know it will WOW you, and you will begin to WOW yourself with what you learn from my experiences. You can be a WOWSER, too!

How do you become a WOWSER?

I am going to tell you how. I am going to share food for thought, action words, motivation questions, and insider secrets to keep you going. But remember, it starts with YOU.

FOOD FOR THOUGHT

This section will be used to dig deeper and to help you explore you. I will rate myself (yes, you get a chance to see what makes me uniquely me), and then I will encourage you to do the same for yourself.

When was the last time you WOWed yourself? Rate yourself on a scale of 1 to 10; ten being the top of the scale, and one being the bottom of it. OK, ok, ok, -- there is no way I can rate myself anything other than a 10. After all, I am the one writing the WOWSER book. LOL! I have to admit my thoughts are always extravagant, larger than life, and just doggone good.

Imagination has never been my issue. My issue arises when it comes to action. I am always playing it safe, dialing it down rather than just going for it. I have chosen 2018 as the year for no dialing down or slowing down or playing it safe. I am starting the year by tossing in all my chips, I have my wings now, and I am going to go for it. How about you?

ACTION WORDS

This section will be used to give you actionable words that will encourage you to not only think about becoming a WOWSER, but ACTING on your WOWSER dreams.

To WOW means to knock someone's socks off, burn bright, slay it. So, are you SLAYING? Are you slaying yourself and your life?

MOTIVATION QUESTIONS

What's a book if it doesn't ask you thought provoking questions to get your juices flowing? I am going to ask for some leeway in this section to ask questions that may not be directly on topic. It is said that life's journey is not a straight line, so I might feel that a question will help you move forward, even if it doesn't seem to have anything to do with the section. Still, I promise to try to stay on topic.

I just started a Facebook group, 31 Thought Provoking Questions That Will Change Your Life. I love the questions that I am coming up with, and how the group is allowing me to really think about where I am and where I am going. Of course, I also love to challenge others, so I am also enjoying the feedback I am getting from the group.

With each question I write, I hear from different participants. My questions are inspiring them to make changes in their lives. Respondents are taking leaps of faith, choosing to walk in freedom, being more proactive, and moving forward after being stuck. My questions are not planned to solicit a written response, but to allow my readers to become more introspective. To ponder for a moment where they really are in life and consider adjustments as needed.

I brought my Facebook page up for a reason. You see questions, especially open-ended ones, help us to process ideas, and the right questions can help us move forward.

Since we are talking about ourselves in this chapter, here are some questions I pose to you, my friends:

- How is your life measuring up to your expectations?

- What yardstick/measuring cup are you using to judge your accomplishments?

- How else could you be looking at your life? What new perspective can you take?

INSIDER SECRETS

This section will be used to give you secret information that all WOWSERs use or do but will never tell you.

How do WOWSERs keep upping the ante and continue to WOW themselves? They get away and brainstorm. They turn off emails, phone calls, and let their minds rest, rejuvenate, and rewire, allowing new ideas to form. When was the last time you separated from the world and refreshed your mind?

Everyone has to find his or her own way to refresh and recharge. I like to walk, and I like to drive around with no specific destination in mind. Often I end up somewhere I have never been before. I always get inspiration from exploring new things. If you are not into driving or walking, try yoga or swimming or biking. The point is to get away from distractions and clear your mind. Find a quiet place, and let the ideas flow.

Your Turn: (Wow, Influence and Command Your Life)

_____
_____
_____
_____
_____
_____
_____
_____
_____
_____
_____
_____
_____
_____
_____
_____
_____
_____
_____
_____
_____
_____
_____
_____

WOWSER TIP #2:
THINK (Exponentially)

"Thinking outside of the box is unnecessary when there are no boxes in your imagination."
Matshona Dhliwayo

A WOWSER is a thought leader. He or she can read and disseminate information quickly. She or he is a critical thinker. Clear. Rational. Strategic. Tactical. Forward focused.

I am sure you have heard the phrase, "think outside of the box." Well that doesn't apply to a WOWSER. A WOWSER's thinking never started in the box. Never saw the frame of a box. To a WOWSER, all thoughts and ideas are possible. A WOWSER's thinking is like an internal brainstorming session, where no idea is stupid. There is no idea assassination. There is no thinking of past failures as a filter. There is no filter.

Here are three examples that may help you understand 'WOWSER THINK':

ONE. If a WOWSER failed to act on an opportunity a year, five years, or even ten years ago, if that opportunity comes around again, she or he will not think about the past failure as a reason to not reach for it this time around. He or she will look at it with fresh eyes. She or he will draw knowledge from what happened before, including the reason why he or she either didn't see the opportunity as such, or feared success or failure from taking the chance. WOWSERs only use prior experiences as valuable lessons, but never as a reason to say no.

TWO. WOWSERs' minds are always going, thinking, and creating. It is not enough to be fast thinkers, they are also innovators.

On thinkexponential.com, a blog by Geoffrey Shmigelsky from April 8, 2013 talks about human thinking. Most human thinking is linear -- you walk, you take ten steps, 1+1+1+..., you add the steps together to get to 10. However, technology thinks exponentially, the 10 steps become 2*2*2*2*2...

That is the difference between normal human thinking and WOWSER thinking, WOWSERs deliver on a massive scale. They see duplication, multiplication, and amplification. They think beyond the surface. What most people see as the ending, WOWSERs see as a starting point.

THREE. WOWSERs are positive thinkers. They believe! They believe in themselves. They believe in a higher power outside of themselves (most do, anyway). They know the importance of knowledge, wisdom, thoughts, and ideas. They believe what you think is what you become; what you think and what you say is a self-fulfilling prophecy. They guard their minds from idle and negative thoughts. They spend a lot of time feeding their minds with the writings and teachings of other thought leaders. They fill their minds with positive affirmations. You will rarely hear them voice anything contrary to their values and beliefs. They live their lives with those values and beliefs as their foundation. They are the masters of taking their thoughts into captivity and reframing their minds to higher thinking.

FOOD FOR THOUGHT

Are you a thought leader? Do you automatically think exponentially? Rate yourself 1 to 10. My Truth, I am a SEVEN. I always think bigger and exponentially. My weakness is my line of sight, perspective, and what I see. Sometimes what I see will stop me from believing that anything is possible. Over the past two years I have been working on what and how I think, see, know, speak, and believe. Making positive changes to my way of thinking means so much to the trajectory of where I am going.

ACTION WORDS

Have you ever heard of the action words, 'Put on Your Thinking Cap'? The origin of this dates back to the 17th century, when the 'thinking cap' was previously known as the "considering cap." The website Phrase Finder (www.phrases.or.uk) makes note that a reference to a 'considering cap' can be found in a book called The History of Goodie Two Shoes, "...it strictly enjoined the Possessor to put on the Cap, whenever he found his Passions begin to grow turbulent, and not to deliver a Word whilst it was on." It allowed the wearer to look at difficult problems as three-sided situations with these options:

1. I may be wrong
2. It is fifty-to-one that I am right
3. I'll consider it

I challenge you to think bigger and consider more!

MOTIVATION QUESTIONS

I was blessed earlier this year to be the commencement speaker for a high school graduating class. My topic was, "What You Think, What You Say, What You Do, and Who You Do It With Matters." It all starts with your thinking. Thinking creates a self-fulfilling prophecy. Thinking becomes action. Thinking becomes what you say and what you do.

What are you thinking? Are they life-giving, producing thoughts? Are they exponential, groundbreaking thoughts? Or, are your thoughts putting the breaks on your progress? It is all up to you.

> "Watch your thoughts; they become words.
> Words; they become actions.
> Actions; they become habits.
> Habits; they become your character.
> Character; it becomes your destiny."
> Lao-Tze

INSIDER SECRET

<u>READ</u>, <u>LEARN</u>, <u>GROW</u>. I have met a number of WOWSERs, and one thing that I can say about them is that they are avid readers. In a Huffington Post blog, The Reading Habits of Ultra Successful People by Andrew Merle (April 14, 2016), he mentions that Warren Buffett pointed to a stack of books as his key to success. He said, "Read 500 pages like this every day. That is how knowledge works. It builds up like compound interest. All of you can do it, but I guarantee not many of you will do it!"

A study of 1,200 wealthy people found that they have one past time in common – they READ.

So, if you want to become a Thought Leader-- a WOWSER -- don't stop learning and growing. If you don't read for pleasure, then start doing it now. Read about personal growth, business, psychology, science, math, people, art, history, fiction, and things that you love. Pick up a book or a magazine. Read the newspaper. You never know what knowledge you acquire will provide an opportunity to become the Thought Leader you want to be. Strengthen your strengths, and work just as hard to minimize your weaknesses.

For me that meant going back to deepening my faith through reading the Bible, and minimizing my weakness by embracing fully that, "For nothing will be impossible with God." (Luke 1:37)

Your Turn: (Wow, Influence and Command Your Life)

WOWSER TIP #3:
BE (Uniquely You)

"Be yourself: everyone else is already taken"
Oscar Wilde

In the world of sensationalism and attention seeking, where people sometimes sell their souls for a taste of both, there is something to be said for taking the high road and just being yourself. If your authentic self can't WOW a crowd, job, industry or market, you aren't ready to be a WOWSER.

WOWSERs are happy in their own skin. They exude confidence.

Some people are naturally self-confident, while others need to find their way. They need to dig a little deeper. If you aren't quite ready to be a WOWSER, that's okay. Neither was I until I dug deep, finally finding my footing, and listening to who I really am.

To dig deeper, focus on the following questions:

1. Who are you?
2. What are your strengths? Your gifts?
3. What are your weaknesses? Your flaws?
4. Do you accept yourself, weaknesses, flaws, and all?
5. Are you over-critical of yourself?
6. If you make a mistake, do you give yourself grace?
7. Do you forgive yourself? Or do you keep kicking yourself over and over again for your mistakes and failures?
8. Do you love yourself?

WOWSERs have done the work introspectively to love and trust themselves, and their actions. They know the heart of who they are.

FOOD FOR THOUGHT

Are you accepting of yourself? What holds you back? Rate yourself 1 to 10. My Truth, I am a '9'. Let me start by saying that the leap to become a WOWSER in this area can seem pretty simple on the surface, yet it is very complex as you dig deeper. Do the work. Get to know, love, and cherish yourself. There is a lot of "gook" in you that you are going to have to work through to get to the real you. You have years of family, friends, life situations, and the society in which we live speaking to you and telling you who you are. You also have your own inner critic being a gremlin and holding you back from seeing the good in you.

My process to get to know and love myself started with my relationship with God. Once I understood who He was in my life, my identity and self-image changed. I became more accepting of myself because God is accepting of me.

In addition to asking yourself the questions I noted above, there are some other tools that helped me get to know myself better. They are the Myers-Briggs and DISC personality assessments, the Spiritual Gift Assessment, and journaling.

Understand that these tests do not define you, but rather open you to understand how your personality type functions in relationship to people who act and think differently due to their personality type. These tests simply group people with similar styles, and break down their various reactions to life situations. Our personal frame of reference, developed over time, will also be a factor.

Now, I walk with confidence knowing that I am a beautiful, successful, humble, confident, and a lovely lady that is excited about Takisha and all that she has to offer. I want to help YOU find your WOW!

ACTION WORDS

I love the synonyms for confidence: trust, belief, faith, credence, conviction, self-assurance, self-confidence, self-possession, assertiveness, courage, boldness, and nerve. Isn't that what you would expect from a WOWSER?

I want to dig deeper into the word "credence." Credence is a belief in or acceptance of something as true. WOWSERs accept who they are; believe that they are true people because they live with the centering and grounding of a higher presence; are humble before that higher presence and the world; and walk in the essence of who they really are.

MOTIVATION QUESTIONS

On my Facebook page, 31 Thought Provoking Questions, I ask, "Who are you, really?" This is a simple question that brings up a lot of complex and complicated thoughts as each individual searches for their own answer. Some prefer not to look too closely at who they are, while others go spelunking into the caverns of their consciousness.

Here is my thought on the topic: it is worth the exploration to find out whom you really are. Life and the universe will not fully open up for you until you can answer this critical question.

Here is a quote by Marianne Williamson, which always galvanizes me into wanting to know more about myself, and causes me to move with purpose:

"Our deepest fear is not that we are inadequate. Our deepest fear is that we are powerful beyond measure. It is our light, not our darkness that most frightens us. We ask ourselves, who am I to be brilliant, gorgeous, talented, fabulous? Actually, who are you NOT to be? You are a child of God. Your playing small does not serve the world. There is nothing enlightened about shrinking so that other people won't feel insecure around you. We are all meant to shine, as children do. We were born to make manifest the glory of God that is within us. It's not just in some of us; it's in everyone. And as we let our own light shine, we unconsciously give other people permission to do the same. As we are liberated from our own fear, our presence automatically liberates others."

INSIDER SECRET

WOWSERs CREATE PERSONAS. Most WOWSERs create personas, giving you just enough of who they are so that you feel that you know them. You get to know who they are, but without them giving too much of themselves away. They understand that others can drain them. While WOWSERs are very much "in the world," they know that if they are drained by others that they will have nothing left for themselves, especially their best selves. They are fiercely protective, and don't want you all in their business.

They must hold back something for themselves, for their friends, and for their intimate family. So, when you find someone giving it all away, that person is not a WOWSER. He or she is an imitator.

Your Turn: (Wow, Influence and Command Your Life)

_____
_____
_____
_____
_____
_____
_____
_____
_____
_____
_____
_____
_____
_____
_____
_____
_____
_____
_____
_____
_____
_____
_____
_____
_____

WOWSER TIP #4:
ENERGIZE (Your Space)

*"It's energizing and inspirational
just to spend an hour or two with you..."*
G. Lafley

Have you ever gone to an event to hear a person speak and were bored out of your mind, yawned or nodded off? That would not happen if you were listening to a WOWSER!

WOWSERs command attention. WOWSERs own energy and distribute it to others; You feel energized by being in their presence.

How and why this is possible?
1. They don't conserve energy, they give their all whether they are impacting one or thousands.
2. WOWSERs know how to use their natural adrenaline to get pumped and ready to go.
3. They visualize and rehearse their performance in their minds, in front of the mirror, and anticipate the response of those to whom they are speaking.
4. They understand the different between potential energy (energy possessed by a body by virtue of its position or state) verses kinetic energy (energy possessed by a body by virtue of its movement). Kinetic energy can be transferred from one body to another in a collision.

Let's dig deeper to make sure we understand this important principal. Potential energy doesn't require motion, just position. Here is a great example of this concept from vocabulary.com: "A boulder on top of a hill has a lot of potential energy because it could roll down pretty fast at any moment." This boulder could move, it may move, but then again it may never move. If it never moves, it will never transfer energy.

Kinetic energy is a result of motion. It can transfer energy. Another example from vocabulary.com: "A person sitting has no kinetic energy, but a person running has tremendous kinetic energy; if they run into you, you'll feel the brunt of it." They pass on their energy to you. Now you are in motion, falling over.

WOWSERs understand the importance of transferable energy. It allows them to connect with someone at a deeper level. That person then becomes WOWed by the WOWSER's performance, and he or she wants to hear more of what they are marketing and selling.

> "The meeting of two personalities
> is like the contact of two chemical substances:
> if there is any reaction, both are transformed."
> Carl Jung

FOOD FOR THOUGHT

Are you full of zest, vigor, liveliness, and vibrancy? Do you energize the space around you? Rate yourself 1 to 10. My Truth, I am not quite sure! As I ponder this thought, I am fighting with myself between being an 8/9 or 10. If I can't come up with an irrevocable number, I always acquiesce and go with the lower number. Let me explain why I am in turmoil. On the 8/9 side of things I have been in a job where I can't be full on Takisha. That is a struggle, because I understand that I need to harness my energy when on the job. So I haven't really been true to myself.

On the 10 side of things, I transfer dynamic energy. I give hugs. I love on people. When I speak, people listen. When I walk in the door, people take notice, and I take notice of them. I make eye contact. I am now transitioning to my businesses "Purpose Innovators and Girifriday Business Solutions." I am pretty sure I will meet you as I blaze the trail that I am on, and then you can rate me. ☺

How do you ENERGIZE your life? First, get rid of anything that is dead, and not producing in your life, like toxic relationships. Another big drain is clutter. Yes, too much junk lying about unorganized will also drain you. Toss whatever doesn't feed your soul.

Second, we allow ourselves to create humdrum lives because they feel safe, but this does not create energy. Climb out of your rut by expanding your horizons – travel; get out and meet new people; join a new mastermind group; clear your mind with prayer and meditation; and get moving with exercise and stretching. Get out of the normalcy of your life. Try something new.

ACTION WORDS

From the last section, the words zest, vigor, liveliness, and vibrancy are still permeating my thinking. What would it look like to approach every day with gusto, enthusiasm, spark, animation, exuberance, high spirits, and pizzazz? Zest for life starts with the inner focus of your spirit. I hope you start there.

MOTIVATION QUESTIONS

There was a song some years ago by Brownstone that penned the words, "Taste the fruit of life. Don't stop yourself to wonder why." How does the fruit of your life taste? Are you happy and excited about it? I am going to repeat what I just said in Action Words, a love for life starts with the inner focus of your spirit. Please start there.

> "If we desert the inner self to focus on the energy outside, it leaves a vacancy inside."
> Trudy Vesotskly

INSIDER SECRET

<u>ANCHOR YOURSELF</u>. A friend of mine, Coach William "Bill" Maddox, taught me an amazing technique to get my mind, heart, and soul ready to perform. It involves harnessing energy from a previous experience to energize and get me ready for a new experience.

First, I close my eyes and go back to a time and place where I "killed it." When I was at the height of my game, owned the room, and people where magnetized by me. Once I am there, I experience it all over again: what I felt, sensed, and received from that moment. I anchor myself to that feeling. You choose how you anchor. I anchor by tapping my leg. So, when I have a speaking engagement, I walk away for a moment and anchor myself with that positive energy from the past. Then, when I get up to speak, I tap my leg and experience the energy all over again.

Recently, I spoke at an event after having been in a small car accident right before I had to speak. I was running late. Couldn't find a parking spot. I made the decision to park in a place where I knew my car was going to get booted. (Sound familiar?) As I got out of the car, another car was leaving. I hurried back to my car and I was backing out when, in my excitement, I back into a parked car with no one in it. There was damage, but I had to get to the event. I finally got my car parked, and then went back to the car I hit to try to figure out how I was going to find out to whom the car belonged. I left a quick note on the car, and then ran into the restaurant where I was scheduled to speak.

Once in the restaurant, I dropped all of my things at my table, and went to the bathroom to calm myself down, breathe deeply, and go back to when I killed it. I tapped my leg and anchored myself. Then I went back to the group I was speaking to and delivered an amazing speech. No one knew what I had just gone through. I transferred my positive energy, not the negative fearful energy created by the accident, to my participants. I was even able to figure out to whom the car belonged (a member of the restaurant staff), and I was able to right the wrong.

Does anchoring work? Absolutely!

Your Turn: (Wow, Influence and Command Your Life)

WOWSER TIP #5:
DRIVE (Results)

"Big results require big ambitions."
Heraclitus

WOWSERs have a natural "Driver" personality. They act quickly. It is not about the journey for them, it is about the results. They gravitate to leadership roles. They are big picture thinkers. Visionaries.

Having worked for several "Drivers," I see that I have some of that personality trait inside of me. So, I get it. Why do anything if you can't see results quickly?

Here is where my personality differs a bit. The long-term results (gain) aren't as important as the short-term results (gain) for a "Driver." For them it is important to see things move along quickly. Advancement is key. It creates momentum. They are driven by 'NOW' results. While I am driven by results; I am also driven by the processes that feed the results and allow them to happen. It is very hard for me to just wing it, and not have the proper procedures in place to make sure that tasks happen methodically. It is the difference between shooting first and then aiming, or aiming first and then shooting. Who is correct? Each of these outlooks is a different lane on the same highway, taken for varying reasons.

Why Drive Results? The 'result' becomes the focal point, the vision, the goal that moves you forward. It creates a sense of urgency, builds enthusiasm, produces inspiration, and sparks motivation. Completion simply means it is time to head onward, and upwards toward another goal.

Have you ever heard of the term "alpha male?" An alpha male is confident, calculating, aggressive, has controlled body language, and exudes charisma. That person doesn't have to be male. That is a Driver. A driver of results. That is a WOWSER!

FOOD FOR THOUGHT

Do you Drive projects to completion? Rate yourself 1 to 10. My Truth, I am a "9", but that wasn't always the case. Years ago, I didn't know my purpose. I started participating in all types of things trying to find my way. I remember my mother saying to me, "Takisha, finish something!" I was all over the place, going after money but not doing what I was good at or what fit me. Finish something indeed!

A couple of years later, I stumbled into the project management field. I needed a job where I could work from home so I could be with my ailing mother. I realized immediately that organizing things, and executing tasks was the right fit for me. Driving projects to a logical end was important to me. I have a personality type that is analytical. I am an "Implementer." I am also a driver. I am dominant. And I am a visionary. (I learned this from all those personality tests I mentioned in a previous section)

I went back to school and got my Masters in Project Management. It opened up my entire life. The degree gave my life meaning, and it started to feed into my purpose! Now completion takes on an even grander meaning.

How do you drive results?
1. Take Risks
2. Get out of your comfort zone
3. Plan and create processes
4. Set measurable goals
5. Build measuring instruments
6. Execute your plans
7. Create benchmarks for success

8. Start all over again (Iterative process)

ACTION WORDS

Sense of urgency synonyms -- burning, compelling, critical, imperative, pressure, necessity and desperation -- are the fuel that keeps a WOWSER going. The goal can't be denied. It keeps you up at night, and after you finally fall asleep, it wakes you up in the morning. You mull over it in the between times. You go into "beast mode" to make it happen. What ever "it" is for you.

MOTIVATION QUESTIONS

Are you passive aggressive? There are some WOWSERs that are passive aggressive. WOWSERs can't be perfect! ☺

Passive Aggressive is not confronting something. It is non-verbal aggression. You are upset about something but you don't share, and you deal with it in an indirect way. Like saying you aren't angry at someone, then pouting about the issue. Some WOWSERs have a slight chink in their armor, they seem to the outside world to be extroverts, but they are really introverts, and they hold things in. This can drive them to use passive aggression instead of being honest and direct.

A true DRIVER speaks their mind and feels compelled to do so.

If you are a WOWSER and use passive aggression, stop! To be a true leader you need to understand this weakness, and work on your strengths to move past this tactic.

You can turn someone off by being passive aggressive. You can be straight with people and be non-confrontational. Passive Aggressives do what they do to avoid direct confrontation.

You can also turn people off by being too far to the right or left in your thinking, and demand that everyone agree with your point of view. Aim for being balanced. A great scripture comes to mind, "Be wise as a serpent and gentle as a dove" (Matthew 10:16)

INSIDER SECRET

MAKE YOURSELF INDISPENSABLE: CROSS TRAIN. A WOWSER is multifaceted: bright, engaging, dynamic, an avid learner, tactical, and results oriented. They don't know everything, but they know a little bit about a lot of things. If they don't know about something, you will never know it, and then they will take the time to learn about it. WOWSERs never stop learning!

I found a great article in the Harvard Business Review that will help you identify areas that you can develop. Please read the excerpt from the article below, and I suggest you use the information in it to skill up.

I can't give away all the goodies from this article, but here is what I can share: Skilling up linearly and non-linearly is very important.

Let me give you two great examples. In most movies where the final scene is a fight between the main character and an adversary, there are symmetrical points to what I am saying.

In Rocky IV the Russian fighter is shown preparing for the fight with Rocky by using the most up-to-date, technologically advanced equipment (Linear). Rocky is seen out in the wilderness preparing in the frozen tundra, running in knee deep snow, using the elements to prepare (Non-linear).

In the movie the Karate Kid, Mr. Miyagi, played by Pat Morita, taught "Daniel-San," Ralph Macchio's character, the techniques of karate in a non-linear way. It was not until Daniel got tired of rubbing the 'wax on" and 'wax off ' of Mr. Miyagi's cars that he confronted his mentor. Miyagi had been training Daniel-San by having him complete repetitive everyday tasks. After their confrontation, Miyagi demonstrated what he had taught Daniel by using the actions within each task as a cue to a karate move. Then you saw the light in his eyes, Daniel realized that he was on fertile training ground. He had learned more than he could ever imagine.

Skilling up in school, through professional development at work, or though reading books on various topics are all linear and amazing ways to grow, but it is when you add Mastermind sessions, coaching, and learning skills that may not seem directly related to your goal that all of the pieces come together. Your mind and spirit grow. You are on your way to being a WOWSER.

Want to learn more? Go to the Harvard Business Review, 2011 Issue, "Making Yourself Indispensable," by John H Zenger, Joseph Folkman and Scott Edinger. Read it, read it again, and read it some more! There are a lot of great ideas about skilling-up in this article.

Your Turn: (Wow, Influence and Command Your Life)

WOWSER TIP #6:
SEEK (Excellence vs Perfection)

*I am careful not to confuse excellence with perfection.
Excellence I can reach for:
Perfection is God's business."
Michael J. Fox*

This one is a bit tricky. Seeking excellence verses perfection is an anomaly because WOWSERs are perfectionist, but they don't chase perfection. At some point they realize perfection can't be achieved. Something deeper is pulling at them -- owning and dominating their potential, purpose, and passion. They don't waste time on the unattainable -- perfect -- instead they spend their time pursuing excellence. Dreaming about how they can be better, do better, build on past accomplishments to constantly increase quality and performance.

WOWSERs are always thinking about how to better themselves. They are thinking about how to be better at their work. How to add more value to their achievements. How to give more of themselves. How to act with distinction, quality, and superior performance.

FOOD FOR THOUGHT

Are you a perfectionist? Rate yourself 1 to 10. My Truth, I was at one time a 10. I was a perfectionist. Until fate happened. I attended a seminar, "How to Become a Paid Speaker," and during the question and answer session I asked the facilitator a question. I asked her, "When is the right time to "go for it" with a new company? I had been planning, organizing, and creating all of these things like a website and social media campaigns to launch the company I was putting together, but I didn't know when was the right time to launch. Her reply was, "Out there is better than perfect!"

I had the answer to my questions, and I had to look myself in the face. I was being an over-thinker and perfectionist.

In the process of all of my planning, creating, and getting my masters degree in project management I forgot one simple thing, GO! The best made plans need breathing room and flexibility. They need the opportunity to fail or fly. They need the intention and action of working toward excellence. Of course you want to get it right, do it right, have a vision, but you have to remove perfection from the equation or you will keep planning, and honing, but never put your idea to action because there will always be one more thing that could make it better. You will have to give the gift of grace, where perfection is not required and you allow yourself to fail forward or soar.

ACTION WORDS

Fail. How apropos to be talking about the word 'fail' when I just saw the best quote about success and failure. Winston Churchill, the Prime Minster of England during World War II, said, "Success is going from failure to failure without loss of enthusiasm."

The definition of fail is to be unsuccessful in achieving one's goal. The one nugget that I find in all great teachers is that to fail is necessary. It is a part of the growing and succeeding process that you have to go through before you can let go to soar.

> "Most people have attained their greatest success just one step beyond their greatest failure."
>
> Napoleon Hill

MOTIVATION QUESTIONS

Are you afraid to fail? Are you afraid to succeed?
Ask yourself why.

I have never been afraid to succeed but have always feared failure. How do you stand before people, knowing that they know you have failed and still lift your head up high?

At the end of a trying time and divorce, I found an amazing job that I thought would usher me into a new start and new life. I moved to Tennessee for a high profile job and ultimately it didn't work. I was devastated. I felt my life was starting to spiral out of control. How in the world could this be? I was primed and ready for this type of work. I could do it in my sleep. It was in my gift. Yet, there I stood with the word "FAILURE" crouching at my door.

I had no family in Tennessee, so I called a friend and shared my pain, sorrow and fear of going back in the community. What where people going to say? What where they going to think? I told my friend that I wanted to stay at home, withdraw, and maybe move back home. It felt like that was the best solution, but my friend told me something that really resonated with me- NO!

He said, "You will not recede, you will not go into a depression, you will stand strong. You did nothing wrong. You will walk with your head held high. You did not fail."

I realized at that very moment that I did walk in excellence, but I was chasing after perfection and it was slowly beating me down. It was good to "fail." It was okay to not be the right fit. It was okay to try and it not work out. Me trying brought a number of life long friends across my path that I may have never met if I hadn't tried.

I still live in Tennessee and continue to grow in stature here. Trying and failing was apparently part of God's plan to get me here, in this place where I am succeeding in life. It was well worth it!

The moral of the story: Don't let the fear of failure or success stop you!

INSIDER SECRET

PERFECTION BREEDS PROCRASTINATION. Every WOWSER I know is a risk taker. They go for it. Some aim first and then shoot, and some shoot first then aim, but they all have decided to let go and jump! Each one of them has a ghost of not doing something in their past or not taking advantage of a great opportunity when it came along that still haunts them. This ghost of opportunities missed propels them past perfection to excellence.

Coach Micheal Burt, a prolific business coach in Murfreesboro, Tennessee, once said in one of his sessions (and I believe it), perfection breeds procrastination. He is a shoot first then aim type of coach. To him you have to try. He tells his teams to not get so caught up in everything being perfect because in the process of trying to achieve perfection, you will most likely miss out on an opportunity that would fulfill your potential and destiny. If you believe in yourself and your idea, it is worth the effort and worth the risk to move forward on that idea. GO!

Your Turn: (Wow, Influence and Command Your Life)

WOWSER TIP #7:
ACCELERATE (Forward)

*"You just keep moving forward and doing what you do
and hope that it resonates with people.
And if it doesn't, you just keep moving on
until you find a project that does."
Octavia Spencer*

Manifesting happens in movement. A few years back I read a book called The Travelers Gift by Andy Andrews. All I can say is that it is AMAZING! This book changed my life. It helped me understand the power of moving within a window of opportunity.

After reading the book I cried, it seemed, for days. I was horrified by the thought that I had missed opportunities that would never be realized because of my inability to move. It was like cold water being thrown in my face. And it was what I needed to start steps toward the call of my life's purpose, even when I was deathly afraid to do so.

I won't give all of the nuggets from the book away, all I'll say is you just have to buy the book! Now! ☺

There is a life cycle when an opportunity comes our way. Sometimes the door only stays open for mere minutes, but it might come around again and we get another chance. Sometimes we ignore an opportunity that stays open for years, only to close one day, never to be opened again. Thinking it would be there forever, we never take advantage of it. In both cases, we have passed the timing of the opportunity.

In The Travelers Gift, the main character finds himself in a room with an angel trying to figure out what the room represents. He sees all of these papers and documents. Some of the documents look like ideas for life saving cures.

Then, he comes across a picture of this little girl and boy who look familiar. On second glance, the little girl and boy look like him and his wife. In his conversation with the angel he comes to realize that he is in the room of what never was, the room of the less courageous. The ones that didn't go for it. He and his wife had talked about having more children, but they never moved forward with the idea. Sadness comes over him. He wants to keep the photo. He can't. It is but a shadow of what could have been. The window for that opportunity was gone. No longer available to him and his wife.

WOWSERs understand potential and opportunity can't be wasted. Moving swiftly when an opportunity is discovered is important. WOWSERs jump at the slightest opening of doors. They have keen perception for opportunities, and wiggle through the smallest of gaps toward success.

FOOD FOR THOUGHT

Do you move fast or slow? Do you find that the inability to make decisions gets in the way of you moving forward? Rate yourself 1 to 10. My Truth, I am a 7. I deal with perfectionism from time to time, which causes me to slow myself down with worry. Fear gets its hooks into me. Then it takes a lot of prayer to get rid of the worry and fear.

I taught something that I learned to a women's group recently, which I think may help you, as it did the ladies in the group, and has helped me.

When you look at something in totality, it can seem overwhelming. It is often too much to bite off. But, if you take a moment to look at it one step at a time, the idea or task doesn't seem so overwhelming. It becomes a single step forward. A single decision. A single piece of the whole.

Remember opportunity comes and opportunity goes. Stay Alert. Be Ready.

ACTION WORDS

Momentum is the impetus "force or energy" gained by a moving object. If you keep stopping you never gain momentum. One step. Two steps. Three steps. Each one helps you gain ground, so that the next step is easier. You begin to walk. Then you jog, pretty soon you are running full speed. WOWSERs accelerate their movement. They are always in the hubbub of energy and life. How about you? Are you walking? Jogging? Running?

MOTIVATION QUESTIONS

My last question wasn't rhetorical. How about you? Are you moving forward towards the call of destiny in your life? Or are you at a pit stop? Are you in the trenches of trying to figure it out? Remember this: One Decision. One Move.

"I'm not saying that I have this all together, that I have it made.
But I am well on my way, reaching out for Christ,
who has so wondrously reached out for me.
Friends, don't get me wrong:
By no means do I count myself as an expert in all of this,
but I've got my eye on the goal,
where God is beckoning us onward—to Jesus.
I'm off and running, and I'm not turning back."
Philippians 3:12-14 (MSG)

INSIDER SECRET

<u>YOU MANIFEST WHAT YOU SAY.</u> WOWSERs understand that when you open your mouth and voice what you want in the world – good or bad -- the universe catches the vibration of the sound of your wish, and prepares for you to take action. It starts with a thought, a word, a move. One action in the direction of your desire will create a chain reaction, and external forces will suddenly be reinforcing your positive movement. This is called synchronicity. But you must take action to get it started.

Your Turn: (Wow, Influence and Command Your Life)

WOWSER TIP #8:
DON'T (Play It Safe)

*"Only those who will risk going too far
can possibly find out how far they can go."*
T. S. Eliot

I called a couple of WOWSERs I know to ask them what they thought about playing it safe in relation to their dreams. Here is what they said:

> "If safety is in your vocabulary- GO HOME, STAY HOME!"
> "Play it safe?? Sorry Takisha, I don't know what that means."
> "Excuse me, can you ask that question again." ☺ (He is a smart aleck.)

WOWSERs ACT! They are trailblazers. They are conquerors. If you tell them that the world is flat, that beyond their vision they will fall off the end of the world, they will ignore you and go see for themselves. They explore and find new territory. They are open to going beyond what others think or imagine. They want to see what is really out there. Sometimes they fall off the edge of the world, and sometimes they discover a new world.

A few years ago, after separating from my husband, I was cleaning out my house and saw all of my journals and notebooks. They contained all of these prayers and ideas I had written down about my future. I was instantly upset about the prayers that I had prayed, over and over again, that were still unfulfilled.

I sat there in disbelief that I had written down all of these ideas about books, conferences, and workshops, but they were just gathering dust. I had done nothing with my ideas. I played it safe instead of making these dreams become a reality.

I was reeling at what I was feeling was my failure. It put me in a bad place emotionally. Luckily, it doesn't take long for me to move from being upset and in despair to seeking God about any issue. He helps me find my way when I am lost.

So, slowly, I approached God for guidance. I was not sure what He was going to say to soothe my ego. LOL. This time He came with a force that knocked me for a loop. He said to me, "All the things you desire, all the things you wrote about wanting in your journals require YOU. They require your engagement. I could make these things happen for you, but I won't. I created you to be the force behind these actions. Takisha, it is up to you to manifest these ideas. Now Manifest!"

I couldn't believe that He was talking to me in that tone. LOL again! Yet His chiding me made me realize some powerful lessons. I was created to DO. I was created to MANIFEST. I am meant to use the gifts God has given me. God has told me that I don't have to shrink back. I don't have to play it safe. I have the power to BE. It is ultimately up to me to go for my dreams. It is not up to God to give them to me.

All I can say is that playing it safe leads to not maximizing your abilities. It means not enjoying your life. Not seeing all that you can become. Playing it safe can lead to a boat load of regret.

FOOD FOR THOUGHT

Do you play it safe? Are you playing it safe right now? Rate yourself 1 to 10. My truth, gosh, I would say I am an 8. My problem has always been that I have to see the path before me. I have to plan the path. I need to have illumination to at least see the next step.

As I move into the next phase of my life into entrepreneurship, there are no guarantees. I have my positive thoughts and my fears -- covering both sides of my decision to move out on my own. I have no idea how this is going to end. That scares and excites me.

By the time you are reading this book, I will have jumped into the unknown of self-employment. My job and my income will depend on my hard work. It will be just God and me, and this amazing, sensational, extraordinary, phenomenal business idea that I believe will prosper. It is business and ministry forged together that I think will propel people into pursuing their calling. 2018, I am flying and determined to take as many people with me as possible!

ACTION WORDS

EXPLORE! DISCOVER! Christopher Columbus explored the world with people telling him there was imminent death if he chose to go beyond the known. The world was flat, they said, and he would fall off the edge or be devoured by the monsters that lurked in the sea.

Taking it a step further, how did he know that the boat he was taking would be able to handle the rough seas and storms? He had no idea, no backup plan, and yet he chose to allow his curiosity to take the lead. He pushed past any fear he might have had, ignoring the naysayers, and he sailed off into the unknown to become a household name.

MOTIVATION QUESTIONS

Whenever you make changes in your life, there is always an internal fight -- to stay or go, to expand or to contract. You have to push past your self-doubts, ignore the people who tell you it is impossible, and champion yourself to move forward.

So, the question I have for you now is from my "31 Day" group: "How are you getting in your own way?" Here is a quote to help you (it helped me):

> "One of the greatest tragedies you can experience is to come to the end of your life and realize that your failure to fulfill your hopes and dreams was due in large part to your inability to get out of your own way."
> Lillian Hellman

INSIDER SECRET

<u>REFRAME YOUR MIND</u>. Your mind has a normal way of thinking, how it processes information, and how it does business. If a particular situation occurs, and you have been through something similar, your brain automatically comes to assumptions based on that past experience, and reacts accordingly.

Your mind frames whether the situation is positive or negative based on how you interpret life, your values, and belief systems. Even how you are feeling that day. It all plays a role. Your mind will pre-conceive how the situation is going to resolve itself. And what your level of engagement will be.

Reframing is a way of looking beyond what you feel, and looking at a situation from a perspective of opportunity. You learn to turn any weakness into strength. To see the possible in what seems impossible.

Here is a great example:

In the last chapter, I framed "perfectionism" as a mindset that can hold you back, it can slow you down, it can stop your progress in life. BUT, there are times when being a perfectionist is an asset and not a liability. After all, wouldn't you want your accountant to account for every penny? And what about the women in the movie Hidden Figures? I just finished watching that amazing movie. Every one of their calculations had to be perfect or someone could die as we explored outer space in the 1960s. Being a perfectionist in these arenas is paramount!

What in your life needs a second look from a new frame of thinking?

Your Turn: (Wow, Influence and Command Your Life)

WOWSER TIP #9:
ENGAGE (People)

*"In motivating people, you've got to engage their
minds and their hearts.
I motivate people, I hope, by example - and perhaps by excitement,
by having productive ideas to make others feel involved."
Rupert Murdoch*

Let's start this chapter by looking at the highest office in the land, the presidency. No matter what side of the line you are on, left or right, Democrat or Republican, liberal or conservative, the last four people we have voted in as president have been incredible. It has been amazing to watch how Bill Clinton, George W. Bush, Barack Obama, and Donald Trump have each defined the job. They have each embraced the presidency, and their run for it, in very different ways.

I am learning that charisma and the air of authority can't really be taught. You either have it or you don't. With all the perceived issues and obstacles each of these candidates faced while they were running for president, and after they took office, they were still able to engage their base of voters in a way that people listened and believed in them enough to vote for them. Although they are all very different, some polar opposites, they have each found their own way of leading and people follow.

In the Bible, Jesus walked up to some of his potential disciples as they were cleaning their nets, and said, "follow me." They stopped everything they were doing and followed. No questions asked.

A WOWSER is a high impact person. He or she is compelled to a higher calling. It becomes less about them, and more about the people they can influence and help. When I think of a WOWSER, I think of the E.F. Hutton commercial from the 1990's when the young professional at a dinner party says, "When E. F. Hutton talks, people listen." And the party goes still, hanging on his next word.

FOOD FOR THOUGHT

Are you talking to yourself? Or are people listening to your message? Rate yourself 1 to 10. My truth? You tell me. If you are reading this book then I believe it is a "10" as I am engaging with you through your interaction with it. My first book, A Lady in Waiting, really allowed me to express myself in ways that I never thought possible. My experiences spoke to others. They embraced my ideas.

I gave of myself and told truths that exposed my life. No topics were off limits. I received wonderful feedback from all of you. It makes me smile that I could engage at that level and be received positively.

A Lady in Waiting made me realize that, even if it had not been received in a positive manner, it was my story to tell. I was not writing with what my readers might think in mind. True engagement starts with stepping out there into the spotlight and giving of yourself. When you share your struggles, you can help others see that they are not alone. It creates a bond, a connection.

ACTION WORDS

Captivate means to attract and hold the interest and attention of others. To charm.

One person who captivated the world was Nelson Mandela. Born into the Thembu royal family, Mandela became engaged in political activity in 1943 by joining the African National Congress.

When apartheid, a form of institutionalized segregation that favored whites in South Africa, was instituted in 1948, he resolved to be a part of the movement to overthrow the government. He engaged people with his strength, and his perseverance, as he worked to right something he felt was very wrong. He initially captured the hearts and minds of the entire world in 1952 as a part of the anti-apartheid Defiance Campaign. In 1962, he was sentenced to life in prison for his activities, but was freed 27 years later.

He risked even more with his speech, "I am prepared to die." As he stood at the docket during his trial he spoke for three hours in defense of his beliefs, ending with:

"During my lifetime I have dedicated my life to this struggle of the African people.
I have fought against white domination,
and I have fought against black domination.
I have cherished the ideal of a democratic and free society
in which all persons will live together in harmony and with equal opportunities.
It is an ideal for which I hope to live for and to see realized.
But, My Lord, if it needs be, it is an ideal for which I am prepared to die."

Even in prison he could not be put down, and he continued to fight for equality for all in South Africa from his cell.

In the end, his dream became reality. The regime that wanted to kill him, toppled, and he was voted the first black president of South Africa. He became known as the "Father of the Nation" for his efforts at bringing both blacks and whites together to create a democratic government that treated all equally. Upon his release from prison, he worked with his tormentors to break down the inequalities through give and take, for which he received the Nobel Peace Prize.

He held the interest of people all his life. That is who he was. He was dedicated to the heart of his people, and the call of duty to serve them. He is a hallmark of history.

MOTIVATION QUESTIONS

Are you a hallmark to your family, friends, and community? Do you see a need in your community that you can work to rectify? What can you do to make a difference? What legacy are you leaving?

> "It always seems impossible, until it is done."
> Nelson Mandela

INSIDER SECRET

The best-kept secret for those who wish to learn how to engage others is not a secret at all. It is an international institution -- Toastmasters International! Toastmasters is a great place to hone your presentation and speaking skills, build confidence, learn how to engage people, and take advantage of networking opportunities.

WOWSERs know how to communicate. They get their point across. They are masters at getting attention and engaging their audience.

Your Turn: (Wow, Influence and Command Your Life)

WOWSER TIP #10:
LOSE (to Win)

*"The will to win, the desire to succeed,
the urge to reach your full potential...
these are the keys that will unlock the door
to personal excellence."*
Confucius

WOWSERs don't lose; they get better. They believe that failure is not loss; it is a training ground. Failure teaches them to grow and mature in their leadership. So, ultimately, they WIN.

Ever thought about failure in that way?

When WOWSERs are on the training ground -- that period between a failure and their next risk -- they vow to never experience the feeling of failure again. Then they work to improve themselves, so they will never make the same mistake again.

I saw a documentary on Kobe Bryant; every game he played seriously. He blamed himself for each team loss. So, during the next game after that loss, he blasted the competition.

Two points to make here:

1. He was shooting down a different team that had nothing to do with his loss. He took his vengeance out on anyone in his path. Some would say that is not a really nice thing to do – seek vengeance -- but there are people that are wired with a passion to win. When they lose, they feel vengeance is all they have left.

    Sports and business can both bring out the best and worst of us. Then there is this gray area of vengeance where we cheer for Kobe and call him the "Silent Assassin."

    Losing is a breeding ground for a number of emotions: hurt, pain, cowardice, and boldness. The point to be made here is that losing caused him to dig deep within and push himself to another dimension of Kobe, so in losing he was really winning.

Karen Hall, PhD, in her article Revenge: Will You Feel Better on psychologytoday.com, says, "The struggle with revenge is centuries old. Shakespeare said, 'If you prick us do we not bleed? If you tickle us, do we not laugh? If you poison us, do we not die? And if you wrong us, shall we not revenge?' Shakespeare clearly thought revenge was as normal and predictable as the sun rising." Hall goes on to say that we must learn from our actions to feel good, Kobe's form of vengeance drives him to play better basketball by making him see how to perform at a higher level.

2. The time between the loss and the next game he considered his training ground. He practiced two, three, four times a day to augment his talent. He watched tapes of the losing game. He stayed after games and practiced. He woke up at two or three o'clock in the morning to practice. He channeled losing into growing his knowledge of the game, building his skills, and enhancing opportunity.

FOOD FOR THOUGHT

Do you consider losing WINNING? Rate yourself 1 to 10. My Truth, I am a 7, I am like Kobe Bryant in that I hate losing. If I feel losing coming on, I can go into a tailspin and go deep inside of myself.

Earlier I mentioned the terms cowardice or boldness and the potential of losing can cause you to do one of two things: run for the hills (flight) or stand your ground and not care about the results (fight). For me the fighting is like Kobe's vengeance. This is one issue that I must truly work on. So how do I change my perception about losing? I REFRAME!

Remember, challenge the status quo of your thoughts; change your frame of thinking from loss to opportunity to grow, build, and enhance your skills. Solve your problem by stepping away and brainstorming possible solutions, then get back to it. You can allow yourself to get mired in self-pity, or you can kick it and move on.

ACTION WORDS

Audacity means intrepid boldness, fearless, adventurous, being undaunted, unshrinking, daring, dynamic, and spirited. I love this word. It means that a WOWSER has an incredible and uncommon way of thinking and moving throughout this world.

Success is all in how you think. I go back to the previous concepts I have discussed: linear/non-linear, loss/opportunity, and flight/fight.

> "From the neck up is where you win or lose the battle.
> It's the art of war.
> You have to lock yourself in and strategize your mindset.
> That's why boxers go to training camps:
> to shut down the noise and really zone in."
> Anthony Joshua

MOTIVATION QUESTIONS

How audacious are you?

>"Let's make sure we're audacious enough to not leave anything on the table."
>Mellody Hobson

This quote resonates with me right now! It speaks of the times when you feel like you haven't gone for it and you are not fulfilling potential, then you finally "get it "and respond to your life's calling. You determine in your mind, heart, and soul that you will leave nothing on the table. That you will do what it takes to make your dreams come true. I absolutely understand why a caged bird sings!

>"The caged bird sings with a fearful trill,
>of things unknown, but longed for still,
>and his tune is heard on the distant hill,
>for the caged bird sings of freedom."
>Maya Angelou

INSIDER SECRET

<u>DON'T QUIT</u>. Ok, I keep finding these amazing articles that substantiate what I am saying to you. Here is another one:

On the Success website (https://www.success.com/blog), I found a blog entitled, "A Success Story of 9,529 Failures" by Tom Corley.

He wrote the article based on his first book, Rich Habits. To write the book, he researched the daily habits of the rich and the poor for five years. In the article he documented the journey that he took through all the failures he experienced on the way to successfully completing his book.

The one constant amid all of the failure was that HE NEVER STOPPED! He never gave up! What can you learn from his more than ninety-five hundred failures? Don't QUIT!

I want you to go and read the article, so I am only going to give you one of the failures he mentioned. After asking 144 literary agents to help him find a publisher, only 30 responded. They all said, "No thanks." Instead of quitting, he pursued publishers directly. When that didn't work, HE SELF-PUBLISHED!

I want to drive this home once again -- linear/non-linear, loss/opportunity, flight/fight- -- there is always an answer to the most difficult of situations. All you need do is seek it out.

Your Turn: (Wow, Influence and Command Your Life)

WOWSER TIP #11:
EXECUTE (Your Vision)

*"I've learned that fear limits you and your vision.
It serves as blinders to what may be just a few steps
down the road for you. The journey is valuable,
but believing in your talents, your abilities,
and your self-worth can empower you to walk down
an even brighter path. Transforming fear into freedom –
how great is that?"*
Soledad O'Brien

As I started to write this chapter, one of my WOWSERs walked into the room, my Aunt Gloria Bromell-Tinubu. She has been blazing trails for as long as I can remember. Her trailblazing began by becoming the first African American woman to receive a Master's Degree in Agricultural Economics from Clemson University, and she broke another barrier when she became the first African American to receive a PhD there in Applied Economics. She went on to become a tenured professor at Spelman College, where she was the chair of the economics department.

She got involved in politics, serving on the Atlanta City Council, Georgia General Assembly, and she also ran for Mayor of Atlanta.

Then she walked away from all of that to return to South Carolina to give back to her community and to work with small businesses, helping owners learn how to run them more efficiently. Once home, she got involved in politics again. She became the first African American woman to win her party's nomination for Congress in South Carolina.

She has since affected change where she grew up by working with the city as a board member of two community development organizations. She has always astounded me. Who better to ask about execution of a vision and making ideas a reality!

When she arrived, I had been writing about how most people's ideas don't see the light of day. She reviewed my work, and I was amazed to see that she agreed with my insights on the percentages of people who actually move ideas to action.

You see, we kill our little darlings in their infancy stages by our inability to see beyond ourselves. We lack trust in ourselves. We see from a prism of self-doubt, emotional deficit, and lack of patience with ourselves. If an idea gets through, and it is written down on paper, it has a 10 percent probability of being acted upon. If you take the written idea and create a plan of attack for your idea, it has a 50 percent chance of you acting upon it. If you put legs to the plan and start acting on it, like exploring resources, there is an 80 percent chance of the idea being fully executed.

A plan is just a written note, an idea that amounts to nothing without action.

I asked my Aunt Gloria what it takes to bring an idea through all of the stages and into 100 percent full execution? What intangibles? She said, "Purpose from God, belief in what you are doing, and its ability to make positive change, willingness to persevere, resilience, and being able to see the end at the beginning."

FOOD FOR THOUGHT

Do you allow your ideas to grow and develop? Rate yourself 1 to 10. My Truth, I am a 10, I love seeing my ideas come to life. I had to learn how to turn my thoughts into action, but I have since taught others what I had to learn the hard way (sometimes it took a number of lessons).

Don't narrow your ideas, let them come: give them the opportunity to exist without filtering them with what you believe can be. You never really know what is possible until you try your ideas out. Let them exist. Add to them over time.

We are our harshest critics. I know you have some amazing ideas, you have been offered excellent opportunities, hold on to them, allow yourself to get past what you consider to be your shortcomings. Write down your ideas, create a plan, and most of all, take action!

I found the mantra below online when I looked up fear quotes. The writer of the quote, Frank Herbert developed the Dune science fiction series of books. He totally understands how fear can block action, and how we must overcome our fears to move forward.

> "I must not fear. Fear is the mind-killer.
> Fear is the little death that brings total obliteration.
> I will face my fear.
> I will permit it to pass over me and through me.
> And when it has gone past
> I will turn the inner eye to see its path.
> Where the fear has gone there will be nothing.
> Only I will remain."

ACTION WORDS

Having my Masters Degree in Project Management, I find myself attracted to the synonyms for execution. These are words that really excite me because they are buzzwords in my industry. The synonyms are: implementation, commission, operation, application, dispatch, enactment, and fulfillment.

There is a saying that losing weight is 80 percent diet and 20 percent exercise. In seeing a dream fulfilled, 80 percent is the thought and planning that is part of the creating. But in spite of all the planning, if you don't move, act, and execute, it will all be for naught. You can get within 80 percent of bringing an amazing idea into existence, then experience "FAILURE TO LAUNCH."

MOTIVATION QUESTIONS

What has failed to launch in your life? What are you going to do about it?

Here are some ideas that work for me:

- Get out of your head!
- Hear no evil/speak no evil: don't listen to naysayers and don't become a naysayer.
- Give your ideas a place to thrive.
- When no one believes, you believe!
- You aren't really alone. When you look outside yourself, you will see that there are people around you ready to help you breathe life into your dream.

Here is a quote that guides me and helps me keep going whatever the circumstance:

"Don't ever let someone tell you that you can't do something.
Not even me. You got a dream, you gotta protect it.
When people can't do something themselves
they're gonna tell you that you can't do it.
You want something, GO GET IT PERIOD!"
Chris Gardner, The Pursuit of Happyness

INSIDER SECRET

MASTERMINDS. I have heard this saying by Jim Rohn many times, -- you are the average of the five people you most associate with. They shape who you are. You, at times, talk like them, and think like them. WOWSERs have Masterminds. WOWSERs also seek out people who are larger than they are, mentors who are more experienced. Always look up, skill up, reach up, and climb up. Share your ideas with higher thinking people, they won't discount your ideas, but will help you develop them.

My time with my Aunt Gloria was amazing, I hadn't seen her in years, and in she walks to give my ideas wings. She gave me advice that elevated my thinking. I walk assured of my thoughts, ready to take the next steps in my journey. She was an example of synchronicity, as you take action on your path, the right people will be there to move you along when you least expect them.

Your Turn: (Wow, Influence and Command Your Life)

WOWSER TIP #12:
WOW (God)

"I'm most proud of the blessings that God has bestowed upon me, in my life. He's given me the vision to truly see that you can fall down, but you can still get back up.
Hopefully I'll learn from my mistakes
and have the opportunity to strengthen and improve the next thing I do."
Martin Lawrence

I have thought a lot about this topic of WOWing God.

Is there a way to WOW Him when He knows everything that is going to happen anyway? As I was praying about it, the parable of the talents came to my mind.

In this example, Jesus is telling a story of a man going on a journey, and entrusting his servants with his property. He gives five talents to one servant, to another two talents, and to the third one talent. Then he went away. The servant with five talents traded with them, and made five talents more. The person that had two talents made two talents more. But the person who had one talent dug in the ground and hid his talent.

Time passed. The master came back, and he was ready to settle his accounts. He saw that the servant whom he had given five talents increased his wealth by five more talents. The one whom he gave two talents, also doubled his initial investment. However, the person with one talent nervously explained why he hadn't produced any additional talents. He said that he was afraid and hid his talent. The master called him a wicked and slothful servant, stating that he should have invested his master's money with the bankers, and, at his returning, the master should have received his original investment in the servant plus interest. So he took the talent from the lazy servant and gave it to him who had ended up with ten talents.

Going back through that scripture, I want to share with you what the master said to his servants that doubled the talents they had been given. He said to them, "Well done, good and faithful servants. You have been faithful over a little; I will set you over much. Enter into the joy of your master. (Mathew 25:23)

As I started to really delve into this story, I realize that we can WOW God by not taking that over which He has given us dominion -- territory, gifts, and life – for granted. We must live life to the fullest.

There is a big expanse out there waiting for us to conquer. I love the thought of God saying, "Enter into the joy of your master." By WOWing God, we get the amazing gift of unspeakable joy.

In chapter two, I stated that WOWSERs think exponentially, and here I want to say that they DO exponentially, too. The servant with the five talents went out immediately upon receiving them to multiple what he had been given.

FOOD FOR THOUGHT

Are you WOWing God with your life? Rate yourself 1 to 10. My truth, I am a 9 ½. WOWing myself and WOWing God has been a steady progression.

I made a choice about three years ago that I was going to go for it, but I still had to go through the process of renewing my mind and understanding that God loved me no matter what. I also had to learn to love myself. Now, I am in this big frontier of my thoughts, and I am matching them to my actions.

The pieces are coming together now -- what we talked about earlier, synchronicity --- and it is an amazing feeling to be truly authentic and living my Truth.

ACTION WORDS

JOY, JOYS, JOYED, JOYING! Yes, it is a verb! I can't let that word go right now.

<u>Enter into the joy</u> (delight, great pleasure, exhilaration, gladness, exuberance, glee, jubilation, rapture, euphoria, ecstasy, happiness) <u>of your master</u>.

As I am fulfilling my purpose, I am stepping into the unknown, and I feel all of the dimensions of joy. Fear is there as well, but, as Kirk Franklin says in his album called Hello Fear, "I recognize that you are there Fear, so hello, but you will not determine what I do and how I do it. I can feel JOY even though you are with me. I am excited that I get to co-labor, and work with God in JOY. That He has offered me the opportunity to 'Enter into JOY' with Him as I fulfill my life's purpose."

WOWSERs are in continuous, perpetual JOYING! They walk life on purpose.

MOTIVATION QUESTIONS

Are you one of the 70% that don't know their purpose? Are you one of the 20% that has an idea of your purpose, but the unknown gets in the way? Are you one of the 5% walking in purpose, primed and ready to go for it, but you still need some help getting there? OR are you living life no holds barred? Are you using your talents to their fullest? Are you living in continuous, perpetual JOY?

I could keep on going with the questions, but I think you know where I am going. Understanding where you are in the continuum of the above. It is very important. Take a moment, look in your mirror, and figure it out. Don't let the end of your life be the place where you ask yourself these important questions. You don't want to die regretting what you didn't achieve.

Exploring who you are, and what you are here to do, is an exciting part of your life.

ENJOY the process and get going.

INSIDER SECRET

JOY, JOYS, JOYED, JOYING- this is all on you. You get to choose. You can choose to live vibrantly, brilliantly, and on purpose.

WOWSERs across the world are WOWing themselves, the world, and God. They amplify, explore themselves, energize people, drive and excel in what they do, manifest, go for it in the face of adversity, engage their followers, lose to win, execute and experience JOY!

> "JOY is prayer, JOY is strength,
> JOY is a net of love by which you can catch souls.
> She/He gives most who gives with JOY."
> Mother Teresa

Your Turn: (Wow, Influence and Command Your Life)

AFTERWORD

"Never surrender your hopes and dreams to the fateful limitations others have placed on their own lives. The vision of your true destiny does not reside within the blinkered outlook of the naysayers and the doom prophets. Judge not by their words, but accept advice based on the evidence of actual results. Do not be surprised should you find a complete absence of anything mystical or miraculous in the manifested reality of those who are so eager to advise you. Friends and family who suffer the lack of abundance, joy, love, fulfillment and prosperity in their own lives really have no business imposing their self-limiting beliefs on your reality experience."
— Anthon St. Maarten

Hi My Friend,

So, what do you think now? How much did this book help you? What one concept can you take away with you right now and start the journey to becoming "your form" of what the word WOWSER represents?

I realize that every person will have a different version of a WOWSER. Each WOWSER has different weaknesses and strengths. I can tell you what to do, to head towards being a WOWSER, but how YOU apply my principals is up to you.

That is the linchpin of this book -- it is all up to you. You get to self-access, go at your own pace, and start to transform your mind and life.

Here are two more questions for you to think about. How will you do it? How will you go for it?

Let me tell you where I am right now. I am standing with a broad expanse in front of me, less than five days away from being completely out on my own. I see a million possibilities before me. I am super excited, and have butterflies in my stomach.

I ask myself, "Can I really do this?"

When I feel the pause of fear, I walk away from my computer, find a mirror, look myself square in the eye, and say, "YOU WERE MADE FOR THIS!"

I know you were made for that which is calling you, as my entrepreneurship is calling me.

Up, up and away we go!

I hope to meet you on the trail.

Blessings and Much Love,

Takisha

About the Author

Takisha Bromell is a Nashville area, award-winning Toastmaster, motivational speaker, and entrepreneur. She is happiest when using her strengths to help others see and pursue their dreams.

In 2016, Bromell founded Purpose Innovators, a company focused on coaching, speaking, and training. Two years later, she left her position as the Director of Client Engagement at Micheal Burt Enterprises to create Girlfriday, a business services and project management company. She is the former Chief Operating Officer for McKnight Advisory Group.

Her first book, A Lady in Waiting, allowed Bromell to discover the gift of expressing herself through the written word. It allowed her to develop the ideas about the "purpose innovator" that she speaks about. Wowser is Bromell's second book.

To learn more about Takisha Bromell, or to inquire about opportunities to have her speak to your organization, visit her website at http://www.takishabromell.com.

Made in the
USA
Lexington, KY